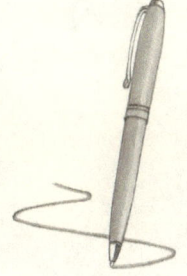

What the ESL:

How I Became a Teacher and Learned Along the Way

A teacher's memoir of insights and reflections from
real-world adult ESL classrooms

Written and Illustrated by Melanie Graysmith
Punctuation! Press

Illustrations by Melanie Graysmith
Book layout and design by Melanie Graysmith
Book cover by David Ter-Avanesyan
Proofreading by Rachel Wright

Published by *Punctuation! Press*

ISBN-13979-8-9998057-0-6
First Edition, 2025

Disclaimer

Author's Note

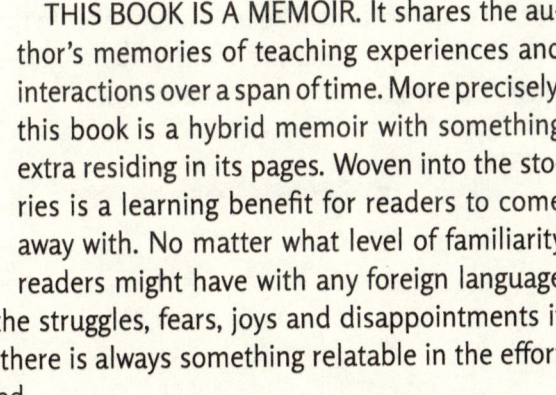

THIS BOOK IS A MEMOIR. It shares the author's memories of teaching experiences and interactions over a span of time. More precisely, this book is a hybrid memoir with something extra residing in its pages. Woven into the stories is a learning benefit for readers to come away with. No matter what level of familiarity readers might have with any foreign language study – the struggles, fears, joys and disappointments it brings – there is always something relatable in the effort to succeed.

The stories in this book reflect the author's recollection of events. While all stories are true, names and identifying details have been changed to assure privacy with some adjustments to preserve the story intent. Dialogue has been re-created from memory and class notes. *Note:* Chapter headings 2–9 are based on several actual student comments and questions to the teacher–author.

The information in this book is for enjoyment purposes only and should not be considered professional advice.

—⁓—

With respect to the ongoing *native speaker* and *nonnative speaker* terms debate, the author takes no position for the purpose of this book. Any use of the term *native speaker* means the language a speaker acquired in early childhood and continues to speak in the present. This book is memoir, shared for insight and pleasure reading only; it is not for standardized academic intentions. To these ends, the author may use native speaker and nonnative speaker classifications as commonly understood.

The English language is so elastic that you can find another word to say the same thing.
-Mahatma Gandhi

Oh God, I don't know what's more difficult, life or the English language.
-Jonathan Ames

The expert at anything was once a beginner.
-Helen Hayes

Contents

Preface

About this book

WHAT IS THE PURPOSE of this book? If you've asked yourself this question while flipping through its pages the answer is straightforward. I wrote this book for reasons larger than the individual stories included here—the snippets of learner experiences I have witnessed as a longtime skilled educator and now share with you.

Let's challenge the idea that all ESL learners come with a singular purpose, or maybe two – to learn English for a better job back home and then leave, or to learn English for a better job here and then stay. Although for each person the goal clearly is to learn English well, it is the *why* that impacts learner motivation, progress, and ultimate satisfaction when they see results and how those results can be used.

This book presents an array of distinct story profiles to further *humanize* adult ESL learners. These profiles, or summaries, are not generic stereotypes but a range of individual stories highlighted here to show the effort and commitment people put into learning English, or any foreign language. While many people enjoy studying a foreign language and can stay motivated, others do not, so there is occasional disappointment as well. Certainly, adults studying English have a desire to succeed, but for some falling short of their goals could negatively impact their education or career plans.

Another aim of this book is to show how ESL teachers often learn from their students. The reason is because ESL teachers typically interact with adult learners on a level of familiarity, particularly in one-on-one sessions, that is closer than with average college students. ESL  learners are likely to open up to their teachers and discuss their work, family, and personal lives. This level of openness is essential to a learner's need for conversation practice in a safe environment to not only practice and learn but also to safely make mistakes.

While ESL lesson objectives for adult learners focus on relevant and relatable topics that encourage motivation, teachers often benefit, too, from some new knowledge or perspectives gotten from their students.

I know of no other industry that would introduce me to such a broad range of people from around the world with such varied interests, experiences, histories, and cultures to interact with daily. Like it or not, English is the primary language of global business and the driving factor of the ESL industry.

As an ESL teacher, I have had opportunities to meet people from virtually every part of the world, including some who have worked in professions and fields of study I would never have had the chance to know or connect with. That reality alone is huge.

Introduction

Why are they here?

IT'S NO SURPRISE THAT ENGLISH no longer belongs solely to its native speakers; it's gone global. For a range of professional and personal reasons countless adults around the world study English, making it the most studied language globally. English is also the most widely spoken language, with 1.5 billion speakers worldwide in 2024, including both native or first language and second language speakers. In spite of that high number just 380 million of them speak English as a native language, a fact that likely surprises many.

Beyond the United Kingdom and Ireland, Australia and New Zealand, where English is the native or primary language, the list of English-speaking countries is long. This book focuses on the United States, where the author lives and works, and the English language learning options available for international learners.

English is prevalent throughout the Americas, with the majority of its native speakers living in the United States. Yet, until recently, English was not an official U.S. language because the country didn't have any official languages for close to 250 years. In 2025, in an attempt to circumvent the legal lawmaking process by Congress, President Donald Trump signed an executive order to make English the official U.S. language. Some states have designated English as an official language — meaning that it is used exclusively for official state matters, which is not the same as English-only laws — as far back as 1920.

Time will tell whether Trump's new order will be reversed and the U.S. will return to its original, equitable no official language status. Due to the country's history of cultural diversity and democratic principles, the nation's founding fathers decided not to mandate a singular language in the Constitution. Considering that more than 78% of Americans speak English only at home, this new order may be seen as mostly symbolic by a fiercely anti-immigrant and anti-multilingualism president.

Another sizable number of native English speakers lives in Canada, officially a bilingual country, with English and French as co-official languages though English speakers outnumber the French.

ele

Overall, English retains a unique place in the world as a language of opportunity with a far-reaching reputation as evidenced by numerous English classes around the world. The current ESL market is enormous, not only in English speaking countries but also globally, in countries where both need and demand for English proficiency have created intensified ESL programs in schools.

According to the 2024 *Open Doors® Report* by the U.S. Department of State and the Institute of International Education (IIE), the United States remains the top destination for international study. The *Open Doors® Report on International Educational Exchange* is the one-of-a-kind comprehensive information source on international students and scholars in the United States, plus U.S. students studying abroad for academic credit. The 2024 report highlights the more than 1.1 million international students at U.S. colleges and universities in the 2023/2024 academic year an all-time high and a 7% increase from the previous academic year.

This is good news signaling the continued robust return of students since the Covid-19 pandemic, along with the Trump administration's hostility to foreigners that kept foreign students away. The Biden administration's 2022 policy changes to attract international STEM students and others began the turnaround. The U.S. now continues as the top destination for international students to study English.

However, in 2025 with the new Trump administration's strong-arm efforts to limit foreign workers, students, visitors, and immigration, the future status of student visas is not known at this time though numbers remain hopeful, but with concern. Within a backdrop of domestic and global uncertainly due to politics, conflicts, and economics, international student enrollment is unfortunately slowing in the U.S. according to data from SEVIS, the Student Exchange and Visitor Information System, managed by the Department of Homeland Security (DHS.)

Note: the *Open Doors® Report* will release its new findings on international student enrollment in the United States for the 2024/2025 academic year in mid-November, 2025; visit, opendoorsdata.org for updates.

What are ESL and EFL?

The term *ESL* is likely most familiar to readers here, and has been used for years while serving as an all-encompassing term for students, school programs, and study areas.

The term refers to *English as a Second Language.* ESL is taught in countries where the dominant population speaks English. It means that the English language is studied and learned as a second language to the learner's first or primary language. Often the second language is used as much as, or nearly as much as, the native language. The focus is to use English in daily communication with native speakers.

Note: ELL is the abbreviation for *English Language Learner*, the term currently used for students learning English as their second language. While the term is commonly used for high school students, it also applies to adult learners.

The term *EFL* refers to *English as a Foreign Language*. It differs from ESL in that it is taught in a country outside the native English speaking countries, and is considered a foreign language within that country. Consequently, English language skills are usually not used as a second language for daily communication with native English speakers. EFL learners commonly need English language ability for a variety of business and travel needs.

It Shows In The Numbers

Adult ESL learners form a significant share of the adult education population in the United States. They enroll in credit and non-credit classes; college and university classes generally are academically oriented and offer credit programs. Upon completion of a university's Intensive ESL program, learners can often transition into the university's regular classes and continue on toward a degree. But not all ESL learners go that route. Many others register in non-credit programs and classes, including online classes, in a multitude of settings, such as adult education ESL programs at high schools, city colleges, community centers, religious venues, and private ESL schools.

ESL School Options

In the United States, ESL learners have two options for studying English. They can attend a private ESL school or enter an ESL program at a community college or university.

Private ESL Schools

There are many independent and franchised or chain ESL schools across the U.S. These schools operate year-round and have varied courses and start dates. Some school schedules are quite flexible and allow open start dates, meaning students may enter an ongoing course at any time. Typically, these schools offer business or executive courses, plus general classes. Overall, private ESL schools are not cheap, and tuition runs from moderate to expensive, with a range of full and half-day class packages affecting the cost. Price also depends on the school brand or reputation and its location. Private ESL school programs are non-credit, so the courses do not transfer over to college or university for academic credit.

There are specific visa requirements for international students who want to take an English course at a language school in the United States, whether at a private school or accredited college.

Community College ESL Classes

Community college is a valued American resource that adapts to and welcomes the diverse communities they serve. These institutions have a broad range of educational programs that are accessible and relatively affordable for local students, opening a less costly route to a degree. Limited English or no English at all is no problem, as community colleges have courses and placement resources for students whose primary language is not

English. These easily available, low cost incentives make community college an ideal place to take ESL classes.

Generally speaking, community college ESL classes are for–credit and non–credit and give class grades. While community college tuition and related fees are lower than at private and four-year universities, the range of tuition varies from state to state. Because community colleges are set to serve and benefit their state population first, the cost to attend is higher for out-of-state students, including international students. Public colleges and universities, including community colleges, receive state funding partially subsidized by taxes its residents pay. To take advantage of the lower in-state tuition, students need to establish residency and show they pay taxes. The requirements for establishing legal residency vary by state, so potential students need to research the facts on this option.

State University ESL Programs

State universities may offer Intensive ESL programs for academic preparation to study at American universities, or for students and professionals looking to improve their English skills for personal and professional gains. Interested students need to apply to these programs, which have scheduled sessions and are higher priced than community college ESL classes. *Note:* not all state university Intensive ESL programs participate in the visa program.

chapter 1

And So It Began

What the ESL Am I Doing?

And how did I get here?

ON MY FIRST DAY AS A TEACHER I simply had no idea what I was going to do. I had no lesson, no book, no plan, no anything — but I did have students, and I was heading off to meet them as their new English teacher. No doubt they, too, were a little scared and anxious about their first day in their English class, supposedly with a qualified, experienced, and well prepared ESL teacher. Well, surprise, surprise, people!

There I was, essentially hoping we could all get through the ninety-minute class without blowing my cover, or the students demanding a refund. Why wasn't I more panicked, more nervous, and essentially more prepared? This learning opportunity, in fact, was what I came to see as a quasi-lucky break, although at the time I didn't quite phrase it that way. Coming up the familiar steps took on a new feel under my feet just by knowing that I was a new teacher starting that day, though I had no idea whatsoever what exactly I was going to do. I tried thinking about it to plan some sort of lesson, which I figured was a prerequisite to teaching pretty much anything, but being at a loss as to where to begin I just let it go. Since I was fluent in English at native-speaker level, I knew I had an advantage over any students who would show up that first day. But then what? What would I do specifically? That was the gnawing question rattling my nerves.

The Japanese Cultural and Community Center of Northern California, where the agency I worked with had its office, was familiar. Not exactly like a second home to me but the closest thing to that feeling inside, the feeling of almost belonging but not quite, of being part of a community yet set apart. Not that I hadn't tried, but not being or looking Japanese or yet mastering Japanese language fluency kept me within the outer limits of belonging. Certainly, I was a familiar sight in the halls and rooms of the building, and now I was taking a step closer to being a part of it as an English teacher.

Never mind that I had no teaching experience or even knowledge of which textbook to use; I was officially a teacher starting that morning and I hoped for the best. Three years of being there and helping arrange monthly intercultural programs for whomever was interested while I studied toward my BA degree in Japanese, were big commitments for me. The floors, walls, sounds, smells, posters, and funny flyers pinned onto the bulletin boards were all familiar to me as weekly connections.

Five young women arrived that first morning and looked equally curious as to what would happen during that first class as I was. But I had almost no idea. I figured we would talk about why they were studying English and what they wanted to do with their language skills in the future, and basically whatever else popped into my head. I was somewhat scared that my novice status would shine through too strongly, so I tried to put on a teacher-like air of confidence.

I had worked with the agency for several years while earning my BA degree in Japanese, and upon graduation, the office supervisor asked if I would teach an ESL class there. I agreed, though I had no clue at the time as to how to go about it. Like everything else I took on, I knew I would figure it out and succeed somehow, but I was nervous and unsure of what I would do the first day I played teacher. I got my courage up by thinking that none of my new charges would notice.

I headed into class with no plan, although five young women sat waiting for their first English lesson. Takako, Momoko, Mizuki, Noriko, and Rieko were in the office anticipating their teacher's arrival. I clearly hadn't been trained enough as a teacher, and in fact had never wanted to be in that role, but there I was in a room half-filled with eager faces looking to me to lead them in learning English.

Momoko spoke first and asked if this office was our classroom. Without a designated classroom for the lesson, I said a space hadn't been decided on yet, so we headed to the coffee shop in the main building of Japantown, Nihon-machi, the Japanese cultural hub. I had hoped there would be enough empty seats for us all; evidently I wasn't the only one without a plan. Unknowingly, I had assumed the agency would have a classroom for us, but it was obvious by then only the young women and I knew we were coming for a class—clearly, we had been forgotten. How do you say "pass the buck" in Japanese?

(パックを渡す Bakku o watasu.)

And So it Began

As it turned out, my fast learning and creative skills carried me through those initial teaching days and even brought on additional private students, plus, most importantly, a needed boost of confidence. But I knew I had to learn more about teaching and working in education, specifically the ESL field, so I could feel convinced this profession was the right fit for me. Looking back, it was a different world then. At the time fewer people like me, someone with no Asian ethnicity, had studied Asian languages, and there were no internet searches or online lesson plans, so much of the information I needed to move forward I had to look for, gather, or create on my own, with few professional or personal contacts I could call on.

I soon began working at a small ESL school, where I got considerably more experience with a range of international students. Based on new confidence in my teaching skills from leading my Japantown class, I sent out my updated resume to several ESL schools in San Francisco. Happily, I was immediately hired by a large school in the financial district with a newly arrived group of Japanese bankers. The school director was looking for an ESL teacher with sensitivity to Japanese culture because the teacher on the job was not working out well; fortunately, my resume rolled in at just the right time. I still laugh at the irony of how my degree in Japanese led me to teach ESL.

From there, my teaching career kept on course, broadened, and–as someone who *loves, loves, loves* to learn, as I would tell anyone who would listen–my merits continued to grow. I enrolled in an ESL master's program (MATESL) but one semester later switched course to an adult education track that better matched my wider interest in the adult learner, including my passion for lifelong learning. I felt there were advantages adult education offered, although at the time I didn't see much beyond my personal interests in language, culture, and art. Ultimately, I earned a master's degree in adult education with an emphasis on ESL, and shortly after added Cambridge CELTA, (Certificate in English Language Teaching to Adults) a highly respected English teaching certification, just because. I continued working as a graphic artist–I already had a degree in illustration–in addition to teaching part time until circumstances changed that pushed me into teaching full time. *Note:* CELTA now stands for Certificate in Teaching English to Speakers of Other Languages. While CELTA remains aimed at teaching adults, in 2011 it shifted to include younger learners.

And So On

Creativity has always defined my strengths and led me forward or sheltered me in times of need. The beauty of creativity is how adaptable it can be. I bring this up because one of my strengths is creating curricula for courses I've designed and taught at several schools, including UC Berkeley Extension's Department for Professional Development, which at the time offered courses for second-language learners; City College of San Francisco Extension; and other adult education venues, where I've taught grammar, writing, and reading classes to advanced English learners and native speakers.

—ℓℓ—

With added life fluctuations and decisions, my creative pull led me to add freelance writing to the mix in the early 2000's. I worked with several media sites as a digital content writer on a variety of topics and as a journalist reporting on adult and higher education. At times I held three to four part time jobs a week, including teaching, which had been an evolving yet constant career.

Through my continued interest in writing I took several creative writing workshops that helped produce a mini portfolio of short stories, poetic-prose, and future writing ideas. All that writing from creative juices bubbling inside my brain sparked my dive into independent filmmaking with the hope of spinning my original stories into film. I joined an independent film collective, bringing along a preliminary script from an original story I wrote a few years earlier. But painfully, I discovered I had so much to learn about filmmaking.

Never a reluctant learner, I enrolled in a cinema studies program at a community college and quickly found how much I enjoyed scriptwriting. The process exposed me to a writing and storytelling style that was a fit for me, and cinema courses offered the challenge to learn more about the steps and mechanics of filmmaking. My love of learning welcomed it all.

Fast forward to now. I continue to be the artist I've committed a lifetime to and a passionate writer as well. I have also tapered my teaching range and currently teach writing workshops. More on the way.

Is It Friday Yet?

The bagels are coming!

MOST OF US TEACHERS WANTED to do something else, while the creative ones were the most dissatisfied. Though it simply may have been teacher burnout, the guise wasn't hidden very well. Looking forward to the weekend was a common topic of teacher conversation. Whether anyone had weekend plans or not had no relation to anticipating the end of the workweek, and some joked that weekends came too infrequently.

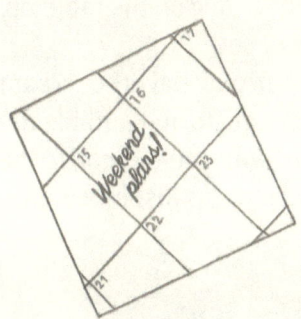

"Is it Friday yet?" was the first thing someone would say each Monday at the morning break. At some point only the occasional newbie or teacher subs hired for the summertime crowd of mainly Europeans flooding into the school would laugh at the well-worn joke. Everyone else was too used to hearing it to laugh anymore.

The weekly Friday goodies in the teachers' room at breaktime ran a close second in anticipation level. If the familiar brown pastry box was not sitting on the tabletop, some teachers would be mighty upset.

We often had bagels and various flavored cream cheeses, which were attacked with gusto and audible delight. A stranger walking into the room could theorize the teachers hadn't eaten for several months just by witnessing the bagel attack.

Days of Our Lives

Off the record

WORKING WITH AN ENTIRELY international group of adult learners presented particular scenarios on a daily basis. Student needs, relationships, and interactions were part of their English learning experience. Teachers recognized and understood this and tried every way to accommodate these high-payers that kept us employed.

Student–teacher connections could go in several directions, mostly positive, although we did get our share of prima donna moments. Over the years a few mostly (but not only) executive types were unhappy and demanding for one reason or another. They had problems  with their homestay or residence hotel or had issues with a teacher, lesson focus, or occasionally another student.

Of course, some students in the general English program could also be challenging, but for business students a lot more was riding on their ultimate English language progress. Students with a natural flair for foreign language typically had an easier learning and settling in time, frequently with an enjoyable respite from the routine back home. But for those who struggled more with English, the experience could be anything from a pleasant break in a fun city, to an agonizing time away from the familiar. In all fairness, particularly for newly arrived students, being thrust into a new learning environment in a new country, and studying, living, and speaking another language each day, was not an easy commitment.

～ell～

One mean-spirited financial executive went through virtually all of the teachers as our academic director tried to find some satisfaction for him, but the complainer couldn't fully get along with any teacher and had particular problems with the females. He whined and bellyached his way through his month-long stay, and none of the teachers or staff were sad to see him leave when he finally finished the program.

Teachers would deliver useful and relevant lessons for students to increase their language skills, in addition to making lessons stimulating, challenging, appropriate, and all around enjoyable, even fun–sounds exhausting, doesn't it?

Students in ESL schools were a mixed bag yet shared many common traits. Since tuition at private ESL schools was generally quite steep, students tended to be largely middle-to upper middle-class or higher. Essentially, students divided into two basic groups: the executive types in the business track and everyone else in the general English program.

In the summer the general program was a magnet for European students, most in their early to mid twenties, who took advantage of vacation breaks from their universities in their countries, with influxes from Germany, Switzerland, France, Italy, and Spain. It was clear that many of these young students here on student visas primarily saw taking English classes as an adjunct to a summer vacation, with San Francisco a top destination.

chapter 2

I Know This Already

Culture Shock

Wham!

SOME YEARS AGO a high number of Saudi students came to the U.S. to study English in preparation for entering American university master's degree programs. Most of these students came as scholarship recipients from the King Abdullah Scholarship Program (KASP), established in 2005. At the time the program paid for each student's education and living expenses while studying here as long as they were admitted to and graduated from a relevant university master's program. Increasing their English skills was extremely important so they could remain in the program and ultimately graduate with a cherished degree. Since then, the KASP has changed focus and been revamped; in 2015 it was renamed the Custodian of the Two Holy Mosques Scholarship Program.

The stark differences between Saudi and American cultural norms, along with the independence offered to and expected of young people in American culture, could be a daunting hurdle for Saudi students, especially for the young men.

One young man arrived late to class one morning with an apparent hangover and clearly was not functioning well. Another student spoke up that his inebriated friend had gone out drinking the night before. The temptation of new freedom away from home and parents, along with alcohol legally available to buy for anyone over 21, proved too much of a lure for young men like this one, who was not used to or prepared for an independent lifestyle.

This situation opened a valuable discussion on personal responsibility and was a perfect gateway to fluency practice and vocabulary building. In this case an awkward situation became a learning opportunity where everyone benefited and enjoyed the class.

Traffic Stop

Now, that's confusing!

É LIOTT, A FRENCH MAN working in pharmaceutical sales, had excellent English skills and no problem communicating in everyday English, yet he discovered an inescapable truth: idioms often confuse. One evening at the airport after returning from a trip, Éliott got into his rental car and started to drive off. After a few minutes he saw police lights following him and heard a voice shouting over the car loudspeaker, *"Pull over! Pull over!"*

Éliott was baffled and wondered, "Why are the police yelling 'sweater' to me?" He knew the word *pullover* meant a sweater, but using good sense, Éliott moved to the side of the road to stop, for whatever the reason.

An officer approached Éliott's car window and asked why he hadn't pulled over right away. Éliott explained he was French and understood a pullover was a sweater. The officer smiled, explained the verb phrase  *pull over*, and told Éliott he hadn't turned on his head and taillights, and they were following him for safety so his car wouldn't get hit. Éliott thought, "Now, *that's* confusing!"

chapter 3

Will I Be Fluent in Two Weeks?

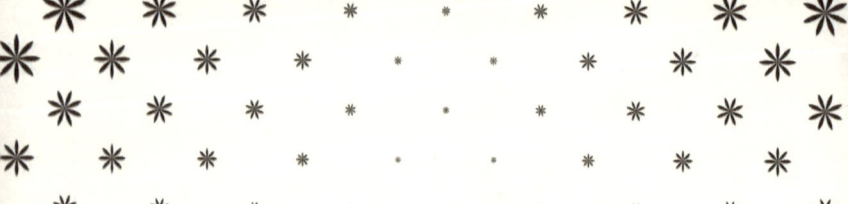

Let's Go!

Playing tourist

THE SAN FRANCISCO CHARISMA MACHINE worked overtime too. Our activities coordinator put a lot of effort into planning the monthly activities calendar of after-school and occasional weekend outings. Students signed on for a infinite number of happy hour bars, free museum days, dinners at pricey cool spots, visits to San Francisco landmarks like Alcatraz and Coit Tower, and bicycling across the Golden Gate Bridge to Sausalito.

The Golden Gate Bridge jaunt, a popular choice, was often a surprise. Unsuspecting but adventuresome students would sign up for the long bike ride without knowing how much pedaling was actually involved round trip. More than a few times a number of students with aching legs after peddling the length of the bridge would opt for the Sausalito ferry ride back to the city—not a cheap ride though a lovely, relaxing one—so they could sit on the ride back and not peddle.

The coordinator had a system in place for each activity. A visit to Alcatraz, the legendary prison and island it sits on, was another crowd pleaser, so many students signed on. Our coordinator didn't actually go to Alcatraz repeatedly, he just had a cattle call of students who paid for their tickets in advance, and he would meet them outside the school. After each student group got onto the right bus and said bye-bye at the Alcatraz ticket booth, off they went, along with one zillion other camera-carrying tourists.

It was best for a teacher to accompany the Alcatraz group in case there were questions and to be sure everyone got on the return trip ferry. I occasionally went along to chaperone a group since the school paid for my ticket and time. It was an enjoyable few hours, although not a tour someone would take frequently since it was the same each time, and students enjoyed having a teacher around to chat with and share the experience.

Surprisingly, dinners at moderate to higher priced restaurants weren't much of a hard sell, considering the cost. While business or older, more financially comfortable *clients* could afford such evenings out (the school and teachers often referred to students in the Business Program as *clients* due to the higher fees they paid) the younger students, often here on breaks from their studies, were more budget conscious. For many students, San Francisco alone was a financial shock, and its budget friendly limits could be a challenge, but with a range of pre-planned activities, everyone could pick and choose which ones worked for them.

Scrabble, Anyone?

No, ~ing is not a word

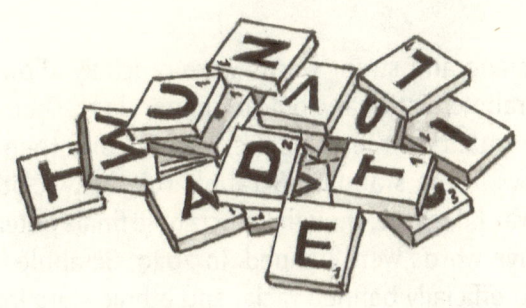

WITHOUT FAIL, every time I asked my class who wanted to play Scrabble, virtually all hands went up. Even students who didn't know what I was suggesting at first seemed excited just to hear the word *play*. I was never too concerned that students wouldn't know it, since Scrabble is sold around the world and in more than thirty languages, so many students were already familiar with the game.

While most students knew about Scrabble and its general rules from having played it back home, almost none had played the English version. With some pre-planning that was never a problem, since I brought my own student-level Scrabble game to class, so everyone could see its board and tiles before we began.

I adjusted the rules somewhat, although less than some students had wanted, so the game remained a challenge with its competitive spirit intact. Students got in teams of two or three, and I let them use a dictionary, though I had to monitor and scrutinize for qualifying words in spite of being lenient. No amount of student protests allowed prefixes like *anti-*, *pre-*, or *sub-* to get by, nor most foreign words.

ele

Most slang and swear words were officially allowed by the Scrabble dictionary, but not in my class. That would be too much for me to define, explain, and then likely disallow. In the standard Scrabble rules any legitimate word was fair game, though for Scrabble finals potentially offensive words were banned. In 2020, Scrabble owner Hasbro officially banned racial and ethnic slurs from its tournament games, and then clarified that slurs weren't allowed in any form of the game. Why did it take so long?

All Scrabble rules aside, as teacher I had the final say. Fortunately, this was never an issue, since the students were there to play the game and winning wasn't the goal.

At the end of the class, when students came away having learned new words and interacted with friends in teams as they practiced English—and had a ton of fun in the process–the class was a success!

The Girl From Tehran

Challenges, challenges

WHILE I HAVE TAUGHT several Iranian students over time, one inspiring and enjoyable experience stands out: working privately with Noura, a young woman from Tehran. Working one-on-one with her was eye-opening for me on several levels. At the time, Noura was studying in a Stanford University summer program and living close to the university in Palo Alto. She would travel by train to meet me for our intensive sessions, initially once a week for a month. From the start, I was impressed by Noura's fluency and ease with the language. I noted her English was almost indistinguishable from a native speaker's, including her accent; her pronunciation was that good.

Noura arranged our classes herself online through an East Coast school that, coincidentally, I sometimes worked with as a local on-site ESL instructor. This surprised me, considering the many local English school options. But through sheer good fortune, Noura was assigned to me. She wanted private classes to prepare for the TOEFL®, Test of English as a Foreign Language, one of the world's top English proficiency exams.

Noura loved being in the Bay Area and studying at Stanford. Though she liked living in Palo Alto, she was surprised at how quiet it was compared to Tehran, where, she said, crowds of people would fill the streets at all hours of the day and night,  even in the early morning. She was amazed that even San Francisco, which she found livelier, did not match the density and vibrancy of her hometown, Tehran.

———ℓℓ———

Noura was a delight to work with. She loved to have conversation practice and share stories about her life in Iran with her family and friends. She said her friends were like her, generally happy and more free-thinking than most outsiders would expect, evidenced by their clothing and lifestyle choices. Noura and I spent considerable time in conversation, in addition to her lessons. However, she preferred to complete the exercises quietly in her student room, as I showed her how to access the online TOEFL® site, including the exercises and study guides, and she had her study book. We would review her answers the following week and discuss any questions she had.

Our classes were in a coffeehouse chain she enjoyed but hadn't heard of before coming to California. She said Starbucks had been in Iran, but closed due to the increased sanctions and pressures set by the first Trump administration. It was the same for other American and international businesses from Europe, as foreign companies were afraid to set up in Iran for fear they wouldn't be able to trade with the U.S. Noura said the sanctions and subsequent business closures angered Iranians. She showed me cell phone photos of a shopping mall in Tehran with stores from international companies, including one tech giant and a famous shoe brand, but said the products now sold there were not authentic but ones made in Iran. She said everyone knew they were fakes, and that was OK, though the counterfelt goods were not any good.

———ele———

I told Noura I intended to write a book on my ESL teaching experience and highlight some learners with interesting stories. I asked if I could interview her anonymously; she was eager to speak with me and give her perspective as an Iranian studying in the U.S., but said I could use her real name, though I declined. I said that wasn't my plan for anyone I profiled, especially someone as vulnerable as she was.

Our sessions ended, and after a few weeks, I tried to contact Noura, assuming she was still at school, though from news reports, I knew the Iranian sanctions and hostile pressures would likely affect her and other Iranian students. I didn't hear back from Noura until about six months later, when she emailed me, which was a nice surprise. In one sentence, Noura said she had returned to Iran, seen her family, gotten a new student visa, which was difficult, and had recently returned to Stanford. She wanted us to meet and had booked two additional lessons. I was happy to see her again, but learned just how hard it was for her to be back. Noura had returned to Iran because she had to, and then applied for another student visa, but due to the worsening political situation, it was initially denied. However, with the university's help in confirming she was still enrolled, Noura was able to return to continue her studies.

We met for a class, but after our last meeting she told me she had to return to Iran again, but would be back soon. I mentioned that I still hoped to interview her, and she said yes, she was interested, and to let her know when. Several months later, I emailed her to stay in touch, as her email address was the only means I had, but she didn't reply. I emailed her again, maybe twice over that last year, but got no response. To this day, I have not heard from Noura again.

chapter 4
Americans Are So Lucky; They Already Speak English

Halloween

Hello Pumpkinheads!

E ACH YEAR WE HAD a bona fide Halloween party with pumpkin carvings, holiday candy, spooky music, and a parade of costumes that drew the required oohs and ahhs–along with a loud round of applause for the "best costume" winner–followed by a pizza lunch and everything else that makes this popular holiday fun.

Teachers and staff were always amazed at how students got completely into the spirit of Halloween, a basically American holiday tradition that had morphed into a bizarre San Francisco ritual. Before the demise of the yearly Halloween  street party in the Castro district, the heart of the city's gay mecca, many students went in groups to view firsthand this famed cultural phenomenon.

It was remarkable how students from Athens to Zurich, all over Asia and Latin America, small towns anywhere else and beyond got excited about celebrating Halloween and came to school in some pretty fantastic costumes. They couldn't get any more American than that!

In turn, students were astonished to see teachers dressed up for Halloween too. One year I came as a beauty pageant contestant, complete with a tiara, long slinky dress, and requisite pageant sash that read, "Miss Understood." I carried a floral bouquet and gave the beauty queen "wrist wave" as I entered the room.

Students and teachers clapped and cheered when the costume parade took center stage. Students talked of seeing office workers in costumes riding to work on buses and trains. They looked at us with an expression of "Who knew?"

Dream to Reality

Keep dreaming

MARKUS PUSHED BACK IN HIS CHAIR as his familiar smile began to expand. It was something so
specific to him, the constant look of awe he had newly per-

fected. But it took his backstories and our conversations for me to fully appreciate what Markus was going through each day in our class. Not just in our class, but also his every moment in San Francisco–or anywhere else far from home–that his middle-aged mind could focus on.

— *ell* —

Markus was my first student from the former East Germany, and what I learned from him could fill another book. He often seemed in disbelief just to *be* in the U.S. and especially in San Francisco, a long held dream location he had never imagined he would really visit. This was just a few years after the collapse of the Soviet Union and less than five years after Germany's reunification in 1990.

For Markus the political turnaround was still vivid and surreal, and he showed that astonishment every day. He would go to the classroom window and stare out at his new reality as that familiar smile began to appear. "Look at this," he said one day as he reached into his pocket and took out a folded, wrinkled piece of paper. He flattened it out to show a picture of the Golden Gate Bridge that he had often gazed at back home, knowing it was a faraway destination he longed to see in person, but likely never would.

Markus could not have imagined doing almost any kind of traveling while growing up in his small East German town. He was born, grew up, and worked under a tightly controlled form of communism–the Socialist Unity Party of Germany—with its rules, limitations, and secrecies; East German communism was the strictest in the Eastern bloc. Its proximity to West Germany, literally across a wall erected in 1961, caused the East German government to crack down on freedoms all the more.

Markus arrived at our school with some English skills, though his speaking was very limited and often unnatural. He tried awfully hard but had little exposure to English growing up, in spite of studying it at school, as the overwhelming language requirement was Russian. I remember so well when Markus used the archaic word "methinks" in a comment and his puzzled reaction at my look of surprise as I tried to stifle a chuckle.

My Arepas Lesson

What's an arepa?

I HAD NEVER HEARD OF AREPAS until serendipity opened the door to this Venezuelan dish for me. The little man with the round face was already seated in class when I came into the room. He flashed the biggest smile, showing large, straight teeth, and then quickly stood and extended his hand to shake mine. "Hello, señora teacher," he said with a slight bow of his head; his toothy grin and pleasant welcome caught me off guard. Whoa, I wasn't expecting that. I smiled back.

"Hello. I'm Melanie. And you are?"

He said to call him Pio, his nickname and the only name friends, family, and everyone else he liked used, so I followed orders and ignored his official name on the class folder I held. Pio was starting private lessons with me, and I immediately sensed that we would work well together, as his enthusiasm to learn was evident.

Pio was from Venezuela, a country then in upheaval, with human rights abuses and violent crime boiling over; he was at a crossroads, professionally and financially, and was worried for his family's survival. He was searching for new work, as his career had spiraled down, but knew that increasing his English ability was important for his future. So here he was, studying English at a difficult time for himself, his family, and his country back home. Our lessons focused on the specifics Pio wanted to improve on: grammar points, reading speed, and above all, conversation—a skill he was always ready to practice with me.

With a lot on his mind while away from the family, Pio would talk about his wife and son, his work, his beloved Venezuela, and the concerns he had for them all. I became drawn in by Pio's ruminations during our lessons together, and with the difficult musings he shared with me. He also talked about another Venezuelan specialty he was homesick for: arepas, a national food of Venezuela!

—ele—

Until then, I'd never heard the word arepas before, but learned they are a traditional dish in South America, especially Venezuela and Colombia. Pio heard there was an arepas restaurant in San Francisco and invited me to try it with him. Toward the end of his course Pio and I went to eat arepas in San Francisco's Mission district, the city's Latin-American neighborhood, where Pio was proud to have me try an arepa–mine was delicious! Traditionally, Venezuelan arepas are tasty cornmeal patties, sliced open, and filled with shredded chicken or beef and various combinations of cheese, black beans, ripe avocado, tomato, salt and pepper, maybe garlic, basically anything you like, though my arepa was vegetarian.

Pio said arepas restaurants are called *areperas*, with many open 24-hours. *Areperas* are popular all day but especially with groups of friends who go in hungry after a late night out, as arepas  are easy to grab and eat. Pio added he'd even seen bridal couples in the early morning, still in their wedding clothes, sitting down for arepas after their wedding parties. We both laughed at the thought of that sight.

A sign at our restaurant's front counter said the place gave a 10% discount to visitors from Venezuela. Pio, happily surprised to see the sign, began a short, animated conversation in Spanish with the owner, and then walked away with a 10% discount on our meal.

chapter 5
You Talking to Me?

The Guys

It's a different world

THE GUYS ARE TRYING TO CONCENTRATE and be part of the class, but with so much funny stuff going on, they can go either way. Salem is a cut-up and bad at hiding it. He's like a number of his friends, thrown into the land of the free, who feel the need to act cool and comfortable with so much freedom, yet voice their commitment to their culture and faith though American lifestyle choices make them uncertain.

The challenges Saudi students face when studying in the U.S. can be overwhelming, on both academic and social levels. Most Saudis study in American ESL schools before starting their university studies here, so the pressure is on. With many critical differences between the U. S. and Saudi educational systems, from gender separation vs. mixed genders in class, to differing teaching methods, student expectations, and participation, many Saudi students have a hard time fitting in. Additionally, trying to make friends with international students both in and out of class can be difficult because the activities these groups do for fun, such as drinking alcohol and boy-girl parties, generally violate the Saudis' religious and cultural teachings. Plus, American legal and societal rights can test Saudi students' levels of tolerance and understanding in ways they hadn't expected.

Salem is under 21 and cannot legally drink, though of course he does, just as somehow American kids under the age find ways. But a bigger and broader *something* with cultural and familial prohibitions creates a more powerful pull for young men like Salem. Yet without parental oversight, advice, and caution these guys could be on their own slippery path.

Drive to LA

Trip of a lifetime

ONE FRIDAY MORNING I asked my class if anyone had plans for the weekend, as I usually did each week. Lorenzo, 21, a university student from Argentina, shared that he and three friends were renting a car and driving to Los Angeles; he said they were all very excited about the trip. One of his friends, at 25, was old enough to rent a car and would drive round trip. They wanted to see Hollywood, Universal Studios, and Disneyland if they could. They were leaving after class that summer afternoon and would drive back on Monday and return to class the following day, Tuesday.

It was clear Lorenzo and his friends had little concept of the sheer distances they were about to travel over that short amount of time, or of the crazy Los Angeles freeway traffic. A few other students had been to Los Angeles; though most hadn't, but wanted to go. Everyone wished Lorenzo a great time.

I gave him some cautionary words to be very careful driving down and on the LA freeways, as traffic was heavy, rushed, and largely unfamiliar to the young friends. They were thrilled to be in California and go to Hollywood to enjoy all the advertised glitter and glam they had only imagined, but would soon experience in person.

On Monday when I got to work I first heard the news from another teacher who didn't know all the details. Soon after the academic director came and told me the other teachers had said Lorenzo was in my class. She wanted me to know right away, before class began, that my student had been killed in a car crash going to Los Angeles the previous Friday; details were still coming in from police, family, and friends.

Lorenzo, asleep in the car back seat without a seat belt, died on impact. The driver friend lost a kidney and the other two friends had unknown injuries. The news was devastating and shocking to me and hard for everyone in the class to grasp.

The Tomás Affair

No, no, don't tell me

THE TALL, THIN GUY was just sitting down as I entered. He had some shine to his face, a sweaty coating from nervousness or having rushed through lunch. I wish I had known more before I entered to be better prepared for Tomás, but honestly, I couldn't have known how to prepare for him.

Tomás was enrolled in the business program and scheduled for private lessons with me. In my questioning efforts to assess his English skills and know how he used it at work, I got short answers, or almost nothing, as he could not hold back the agony he was going through. To say Tomás was distracted from the start would be, to use a cliché, an understatement.

Tomás was from Chile, worked for one of the country's largest banks, was married, and had a nine-year-old son. He was also having an affair with a woman he was madly in love with, a fact he told me almost immediately after a short introduction, adding that he didn't know what to do. Actually, he knew what he should do, but what he should do was not an option. He had been having the affair for about three years, his wife knew, and the situation at home was terrible. This sort of revelation from a student was a new one for me, and not one I welcomed.

As I was unwittingly sucked into this dilemma I asked about divorce in Chile, which he said he wanted, since Chile had recently legalized divorce, but his wife refused because she was Catholic with strong religious beliefs against it. Although Tomás, too, was Catholic he said religion didn't matter much to him; he just wanted to divorce. He was also worried about his son, living in the chaos at home.

I told Tomás this information was none of my business; we were there to study English and to focus on lessons. It was my job as his teacher to work with him on his English, but he had now put me in an uncomfortable situation. I made efforts to redirect the time to a lesson. I reminded him that his job depended on his learning and that's why he was there, plus his company was paying. The more I tried to change the conversation the more sweaty and agitated he became. He blurted out the woman was going to arrive in San Francisco the next day, and though he wanted to see her he also knew he had to make a decision.

I thought for a moment. If we could at least have a fuller conversation in English, even about this subject, I could point out vocabulary, phrases, or anything else relevant to move away from his angst and divert him. Not surprisingly, the plan didn't work.

Tomás came to class the next day, but in a fit to meet his girlfriend at the airport on time he left class early. He never returned, and withdrew from the school completely.

chapter 6

British or American: Which Is the Real English?

Teacher, Teacher

It's polite in my country

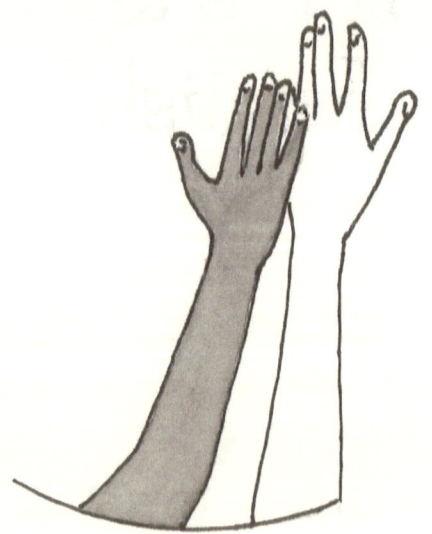

"TEACHER, TEACHER," RAFAEL CALLED to me in that distinctive lilting, musical tone so familiar from my years of teaching Brazilian students. The accent came infused with *samba*, its sound, its rhythm and unmistakable melodic lightness, so sweet. Rafael called again from the edge of the room and quickly corrected himself, a growing grin spreading to cover his face as he restated his call, now saying my name, this time distinctly, with a little boy look of apology.

What is it about English that makes the term *teacher*, when used as an honorific title face-to-face, sound so awful? Why is the term, used as a sign of respect in virtually every other language across the globe, considered rude and harsh sounding in English dominant countries? It has the same irritating edge in England and other English speaking countries as it has in the U.S.

In this country it's been common to say Miss, Ms. or Mr. plus the last name when calling a teacher; it's the culture, though at the college level an instructor may agree to or even encourage using his/her first name. In the earliest grades, kindergarten or first grade, a child might say "teacher" but after that it isn't natural. Got all that?

Word of the Day

How do I say it?

THE LADIES WERE A GIDDY BUNCH, and their time in class was more social than study, yet in spite of their seeming disinterest they actually learned something. The English conversation class wasn't meant to be an after lunch gossip group, but the women chimed in until the chatter was hard to ignore.

I wasn't the only one to let the ladies know they were disruptive, but getting them back on track often took effort. Fortunately, several learning-intent students pitched in to get the slackers to pay attention. Some men in the class who were pretty quiet gave the chatty women a few harsh words in Chinese, followed by icy stares. But most effective were two no-nonsense women who called out to the chatty ones and the room went silent. Essentially I had a class at two ends of a spectrum.

———

This particular day's vocabulary lesson was on words and phrases for physical ailments, and how to describe being sick. Some vocabulary lists drew in more interest than others, and in general words and phrases for physical ailments did just that.

The class didn't have much trouble with the textbook section of small drawings of facial expressions illustrating headache, toothache, stomachache, flu, cold, and tired—but then came *diarrhea*. The word it-

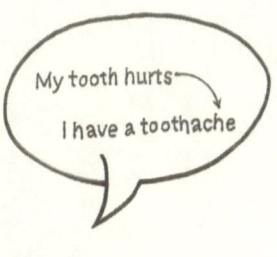

self was difficult for many of them to pronounce, so we practiced saying the word out loud together, over and over several times –di-ar-*rhea*, di-ar-*rhea*, and then of course, what does it mean?

As the teacher I scramble to describe this physical condition, *diarrhea*, without any sign of awkwardness; it's certainly not an ailment a teacher could demonstrate. Funny things do come up and how the teacher handles it, which often takes some quick thinking, comes to the rescue. From two sides of the classroom came shouts of the word in Chinese, followed by nods and a smattering of giggles. They got it.

chapter 7
My Job Depends on Me Speaking English

The Lady Judge

Sweater girl

T HE LITTLE LADY IN THE CASHMERE VEST was unusually deficient in English. While most students came to our school with at least mid-beginner level English skills and could have a simple or rudimentary conversation, Erdene, the new arrival, could barely manage little more than a reluctant hello. Although she was struggling to learn English she was persistent, and tried hard in spite of her limitations as she had a major responsibility to learn. Erdene's unique background showed why she had never studied English or been exposed to it at all.

While most foreign students studied English to some degree in school while growing up, Erdene had not. She had studied Russian when she attended Mongolian public schools and then at law school in Moscow  when Russia was part of the former Soviet Union.

Erdene was a judge from Ulaanbaatar, the capital of Mongolia, and was part of the legal team to amend the 1992 Mongolian Constitution adopted after the fall of the Soviet Union in 1989. The authoritarian government left in 1990 and a democratic Mongolia emerged in 1992, along with its new constitution that Erdene said was based on the US Constitution. Erdene could not fully convey to me just what her role was as it related to the revised Mongolian constitution, but she was determined to prepare for whatever was ahead.

About those cashmere vests Erdene wore every day, if not a vest then a sweater or a scarf, but she would wear something made of cashmere.

When I complimented her on the item she wore she would wave it off like such pieces were common in Mongolia, although she certainly knew their value.

One morning Erdene arrived with a beautiful cashmere scarf the color of deep burgundy that she gifted to me. I was shocked at such a gift from a student, but she was happy for me to have it, and so it became mine.

A day or so later she said if I wanted a cashmere vest or sweater I could buy it through her for a good price, about $200, maybe less. In spite of the good deal I passed on the offer.

The Honeymooners

Memories are forever

THEY WERE HAPPY, EXCITED and on their honeymoon—what could go wrong? The newly arrived young couple had married in Japan just the week before.

Aiko, slim and poised, was a professional ballet dancer and looked the part. Yoshi, a good-looking young executive, was building up his career, and improving his English was part of the rise.

They came to San Francisco for a month-long honeymoon with romanticized plans of Yoshi in English class during the day while Aiko meandered the city, sightseeing and enjoying herself. In the evening they would go out for dinner and have fun at night; on weekends they would enjoy honeymoon things like wine country tours, bay cruises, museum visits, and trendy shopping sprees, or even a few outlet malls Aiko had read about. Yoshi shared the couple's plans in initial class introductions, and his teachers and classmates wished them well. So, what could go wrong? For starters, just about everything.

_____ell_____

In a short time it became clear to teachers and others that things weren't going well for Yoshi. He looked tired and seemed worried and kept to himself during class breaks. English study was hard for him, and along with daily classes came a lot of work: homework, weekly quizzes, and preparing for his big oral presentation in a few weeks, something required of all students at the end of their course. Plus, he discovered that speaking a foreign language for most of the day was tiring, even exhausting sometimes, and he became overwhelmed. He hadn't expected to do so much work, but his company was paying for the course and he needed to keep up. Yoshi had to do homework and study each night, so he and Aiko would return to their hotel room right after dinner. After a week of wandering the city by herself Aiko enrolled in English classes, though mainly to have something to do, but she only lasted a few days there.

Yoshi had to fully focus on his classes as his future with the company depended on it, and it wasn't easy for him. Aiko wanted more honeymoon fun like they had planned; her happiness depended on it, and it wasn't easy for her. Little more than two weeks after they had arrived Aiko returned home to Japan while Yoshi remained to finish his business English course.

This sad outcome was not the first or only time I saw this type of couple conflict at an ESL school. Students often don't realize or understand the amount of time and effort they need to put into their classes, especially when an employer is paying for a Business English or Certificate program, and the pressure to do well is particularly stressful. Students that consider enrolling in such courses should think realistically about bringing a significant other along for an extended stay, particularly if the other person will not be taking classes.

Besides being a time to unwind and celebrate your love, one reason for a honeymoon is to help set the tone of your marriage. A school or work centered honeymoon is not anyone's ideal way to start a married life together.

Tried Her Best

A for effort

DIANA, A FORMER DOCTOR of ten years who half jokingly said she quit the profession because she couldn't stand dealing with blood, was my private student at a biotechnology facility where she worked on pharmaceutical research. Originally from China, Diana was not her real name but one she adopted from a classic British actress she admired, who coincidentally, had a similar last name, so Diana became her English name.

Although a bright woman, Diana found it hard to progress much further in English beyond the point she seemed stuck at, particularly with her writing and pronunciation, skills she knew were holding her back professionally. Diana wasn't wrong on this account, as the verbal and written evaluations she received noted her English flaws, which, fairly or not, were like a brick wall she couldn't break through.

Our twice-weekly lessons were productive on several levels, as often happens with adult ESL learners and their teachers, especially when lessons are one-on-one, as I typically had with international professionals. The genuine connection with a caring teacher has a vital impact on learner attitude and motivation. Too many negative comments can have a defeatist effect on learners, and I saw Diana losing the motivation to learn and ultimately progress in her job. She welcomed the opportunity to safely vent as I listened to her feelings and read some of the supervisor's comments she shared with me.

Adding to her stress, Diana was concerned about her husband and young daughter, who lived with her here, especially her daughter, who, though doing well at school and having friends, Diana knew would have to say goodbye within a few months as Diana would once again relocate to another country. This caused a mixed bag of emotions for her.

For international learners navigating their way through work, English lessons, and family issues, whether the family is back in the home country or living here, means they are juggling an array of challenges. Plus, I have noted that when the learner is a woman here with her family, particularly with young children, the full burden she carries is greater than that of male learners with families here, although men less frequently move with their families. This is true even when men must live and work here for two or more years, which often happens with Asian professionals. The gender gap issue is striking.

When Diana's work allowance for paid ESL lessons ran out, she was upset. She wanted to continue working with me until she left to relocate, which at that point was in about a month. To that end, she offered to hire me on her own for lessons three times a week through her last week on the job, and I agreed. It was a beneficial yet poignant ending for her, both at her work site and living in the Bay Area, a place where she and her family enjoyed many day and weekend trips together.

I often think of Diana via a cultural item she gifted me at Chinese New Year, and it's something I use almost every day. It began as a box of colorful gummy-like New Year's candies presented in a sturdy, white cotton canvas bag with a biomedical science company logo in English and Chinese printed on the front. While the candies were awful, borderline inedible as they were hard to chew and too sweet, the bag, just the right size for me, was a winner and has been a great tote for short shopping trips.

chapter 8

Why Is All American Money Green?

Hawaii Weekend

Plan ahead

FERNANDO, A PRIVATE BUSINESS STUDENT, was a paralegal from Brazil and determined to experience as much as possible while here. One Tuesday morning he told me he was going to Hawaii for the weekend, leaving that Thursday and flying back on Sunday, and returning to class on Monday. This news surprised and concerned me because I knew his vacation plan was too short. I wanted to warn him but he had already booked his trip.

Once he had his tickets he saw the flight to Honolulu was almost 5.5 hours, and the return flight 5 hours. He was stunned and had no idea the flight was so long. I told him that Hawaii was three hours earlier than California to explain arrival times that could be confusing. I then added that flights to Hawaii from California were half the flying time to Japan, a detail that made his jaw drop.

~ele~

The enormity of the United States often surprises foreign students when they first come here. I have seen many students arrive with hopes of visiting several well-known cities and tourist spots while they are here, but rarely have a realistic sense of the distance or amount of time it takes to get from one place to another. I know it's common for travelers in general to underestimate the number of sights they can see on one trip, but students also need to factor in school time, which adds another roadblock to their plans.

Students studying on the West Coast, particularly in California, the most popular state for international students, frequently want to visit Hawaii thinking it is close, quick, or cheap to get to. Then they discover the reality: none of those are true.

Fernando returned to class on Monday with a story to tell, one of disappointment and frustration with a bit of good, but no regrets since he had learned something. Fernando's late flight got him to Hawaii at night, and to his hotel with little time or energy left for anything more than dinner. His room wasn't up to his standards and he saw other issues in the morning, so he left. He had wrongly assumed his hotel was walking distance to a beach, an option important to him. He found another hotel across from the beach but paid a lot more. By the time he settled in and had lunch it was mid-afternoon on Friday. Unfortunately, it was a rainy day so he relaxed by the hotel pool. On Saturday he went to the beach and then took a cab to the Waikiki area and played tourist. On Sunday he had an afternoon flight, so only had time for breakfast before heading to the airport.

Fernando's trip review was that he had one good day, Saturday, found Hawaii expensive, and spent too much time traveling. He wanted to return for a longer stay, but felt at least now he could truthfully tell his friends in Brazil that he had been to Hawaii.

Meet Miki

Clean sweep

MIKI WAS QUITE A CHARACTER – a funny and thoroughly likeable young woman who said the zaniest things, often at the unlikeliest moments. Only Miki didn't realize it soon enough in spite of the quizzical looks she received, and her "What happened?" shoulder-raising response only added to the humor. One notable quality about Miki was that she truly wanted to learn English and increase her speaking skills, so she happily engaged with teachers, classmates, and friends of friends to chat about almost anything. Luckily, Miki was a delight to be around, and a quick learner.

───*ele*───

One of Miki's surprising traits was that she loved to clean – as in cleaning houses, and *love* was the word. When she mentioned that she wanted to clean people's houses to practice English it took me a moment to think about it–after my initial amazement at the idea. Who does that? No one enjoys housecleaning, I thought. An original thinker and eager to learn, Miki said she enjoyed the alone time she had while cleaning her room, and did a lot of studying and planning in her head in the process. Plus, she liked to keep things clean.

At the time I also worked part-time in an office as the firm's graphic artist and webmaster. I invited Miki to meet me there for lunch one day, and to also meet a young woman around Miki's age who worked there; perhaps they could be English conversation partners and become friends.

Soon after Miki arrived she noticed file folders behind a desk, and eyed the reception room to see it all. The next day at school Miki told me she would like to help tidy up the office: do the dusting, filing or whatever else she could, and also hear the natural conversation style people used in an office.

I then spoke with the firm's owner, who was initially surprised at Miki's offer, but after some consideration he agreed. As an international student Miki could not be paid for work, which was against student visa rules and not what she wanted anyway, so Miki helping out in the office for additional English opportunities was fine—a win-win situation.

Miki was innovative and determined, and used creative ways to meet people for natural conversation and listening practice. She immersed herself in out-of-class learning environments and took control of her education. Perfect!

chapter 9

In My Country, Everything Is Better

Riviera Boy

You know... in France.

T HE BOY CAUGHT MY EYE as soon as he walked into the class.

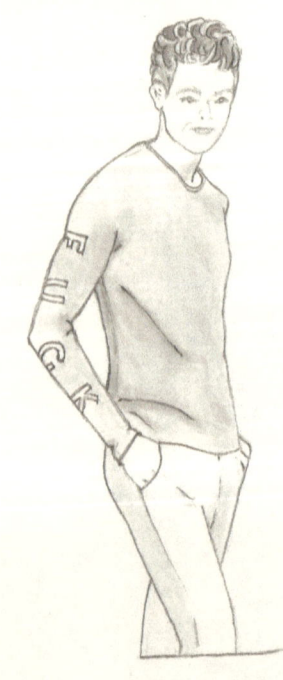

I knew he was French immediately, though at 17 he was younger than the typical French student at our school, even the ones who had recently graduated from lycée and passed "le bac." His name was Michel, which seemed a perfect fit.

His clothing was a giveaway, though I recognized how much of a stereotype I was imposing on him as the quintessential French boy. Michel was trim–no, he was incredibly slim–and wore an attention-grabbing long sleeved black t-shirt, one sleeve pushed up to mid-arm length. The attention-grabber on the other sleeve in large, white capital letters that visually popped was the word *FUCK*. The word marched down the sleeve like a proud logo, though Michel seemed oblivious to its undeniable power as he ignored all the eyes on him. He definitely was a presence in the room.

Michel's tight denim pants, seemingly spray-painted on his lithe body, paired perfectly with his sockless canvas sneakers with their air of haute chicness that he wore so well.

He said he was from Saint Tropez, "in France" he clarified, as if we had no idea. Really, I thought, *Saint Tropez?* People actually live there? Are from there? "Yes" he nodded as if reading my mind, and said he was born there. Ah yes I thought. Of course.

The Doctor's Note

Eye opener

BY THE TIME I MET BENICIO, an ophthalmologist from Argentina, I had been wearing eyeglasses for practically my entire life. With bad eyesight since childhood requiring glasses with progressively stronger correction and thicker lenses, it was easy for Benicio to assess my vision problem as he sat in my class.

Although I had always longed for better vision so I wouldn't need the awful, heavy, costly glasses I wore, I knew of no realistic option beyond contact lenses, which after a difficult tried-but-failed few years of wearing, I had simply given up on.

One day after class Benicio told me of a then new procedure called *Lasik* that was not yet legal in the U.S. but available in other countries, including Argentina. If I would go to Buenos Aires, where Benicio had his medical practice, he would perform Lasik surgery on me, offered at a discounted price. He briefly explained the procedure and its pluses as a start. Lasik had the potential to allow me to see without glasses, or more likely my middle-aged eyes would just need basic reading glasses. I was immediately and totally interested.

Benicio's introduction to Lasik started my research into it, which took some sleuthing since this was the late 1990's, before widespread use of the Internet to find answers. I  briefly considered Benicio's Buenos Aires offer but soon rejected it as surgery recovery and follow-up office visits were not practical, plus added travel and hotel costs made it out of reach.

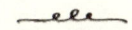

I ultimately found a local ophthalmologist working with the FDA on Lasik approval and considered top in the field. This doctor did my surgery just as it became available in this country. But I will always remember Benicio, my former student who kick-started my life-changing journey and dream of naturally clear vision.

Adulting Can Wait

You're only young once

Buongiorno ESL

I WELCOMED THE CHANCE to work with the teens. The opportunity to teach young Italians easily made me smile. The program overseeing the young students was a well-respected Italian company offering educational and cultural English vacation travel to young people. I interviewed for the job after I answered an ad for an ESL teacher in a summer program for Italian teens in Berkeley, California. The job description piqued my interest and after a somewhat lengthy interview process I got the job, co-teaching with another local ESL instructor.

The teens were full of energy from the first moment they came into my class. I saw the group's keen anticipation for their English program and month long stay in Berkeley, where they moved into dorm rooms on the UC Berkeley campus, a living situation everyone welcomed. They were 13 to 19, and while I occasionally had students who were 17 or 18, younger ones were out of my teaching range. Separate from college ESL programs the minimum age generally accepted at ESL schools is 16 to 18.

Clearly, I was in new territory with the youngest ones, and I could see that from the start. Early on I literally had to separate two boys, one 13 and the other 14, rough-housing on the floor, entwined in each other like a ball and throwing punches as they ignored my commands to stop. I had to pull them apart, not an easy chore, and one not in the job description. Other students nearby who saw this chaos just waved it off with a flip of their hands saying the boys always did this sort of thing. I couldn't let such behavior slip by, and after separating and moving them apart I had them sit at opposite ends of the long classroom table; finally the class continued with stifled giggling for a few seconds more. For the remainder of the course I kept a watchful eye on the boys – my reign of behavior control.

So there I was with a group of young people ranging in age from an impulsive 13 to a mature 19, with mainly motivated teens in-between. I hesitated to tell anything negative to the adult handlers that traveled with the teens from Italy and oversaw their stay and how they adjusted to the program and the UC campus rules. When asked about the group's behavior my co-teacher and I would give broad positive reviews. After all, I had also sensed there was a lot of good for me to potentially learn from the teens. And I did. I have to give those smart young people credit for giving me a keener insight into working with and teaching their age group.

In the first week of class I discovered that most of the kids knew each other pretty well, and many had traveled together before with the same cultural vacation program. I also heard through the grapevine of the more chatty ones that a few of the girls and boys were currently dating. That little fact helped explain the coy playfulness among them, a flirty bit of eye contact not well hidden. The seating arrangement too, I noticed, was not as random as it first appeared, but all was good. Everyone seemed happy, glad to be away from parents, not quite fully on their own but close enough, and excited to visit California.

———

As this trip was an educational and cultural program, social events and weekend activities were built into the plan. These included arts, music, weekend daytrips, and a weekend-long excursion. The group schedule went something like this: weekday tutorials until 4 pm, after class student down time followed by dinner at the UC dining hall or a local restaurant, and then back to the dorms. Weekends were for Bay Area cultural activities: museums, San Francisco theater, Sausalito ferry ride, Sonoma Plaza lunch, and an overnight Santa Cruz Beach excursion, the trip highlight.

I usually got feedback on how they enjoyed the outings, especially to the Santa Cruz Beach Boardwalk, a seaside amusement park down the California coast a scenic 1.5 hour drive from Berkeley. Everyone loved this weekend

trip except one snooty boy who called it "nothing special" and said Italy had something similar, but better. The
others in class immediately booed him and snapped back
they had fun, notably two girls who dreamily said they
loved it!

Berkeley being Berkeley welcomed the young Europeans
in its own renowned way. One morning two boys came to
me, a surprised look on their faces, as if about to tell me
something shocking. They said a man was selling marijuana on Telegraph Avenue, just a block away. The day before
the man had approached them and asked if they wanted
to buy some; the boys were stunned. They said you could
get marijuana in Italy too, but not from street vendors
selling so openly. I could only shrug my shoulders and
raise my arms in pretend surprise. In the end it became
another story for the boys to tell when they got back home.
Così è la vita!

chapter 10
And Another Thing

ESL Teacher Profile

Who does this?

CULTURAL AWARENESS

TRAVEL

LEARNING

CREATIVITY

TECH SKILLS

TRAINING

EXPERIENCE

FOREIGN LANGUAGE

F ROM PERSONAL TEACHING EXPERIENCE, and drawing on my knowledge and astute awareness of commonalities observed in fellow ESL teachers, several distinct characteristics emerge to signal future teacher success. What type of person with such qualities is drawn to this profession?

1. *Cultural Awareness*–An adventurous spirit and love of travel are qualities that most ESL teachers share. By the time many ESL teachers land a teaching job in the U.S. they have traveled to different parts of the world and often taught English during these trips. Sometimes the destination was for an ESL teaching job, though many times teaching was a way to support themselves to continue traveling or learning another language along the way.

2. *Foreign Language Skills*–Most ESL teachers speak at least one other language to some degree, often at an intermediate level. This love of foreign language (FL) serves ESL teachers well, as they can relate to the struggles of learning a FL even though they enjoy the process. While most ESL learners study English because it is required for their jobs, others may simply enjoy learning for the benefits that second language (L2) skills offer, such as traveling and meeting new people.

3. *Creativity*–Being creative is an essential gift for a successful ESL teacher. The ability to create or improve on existing lesson plans, games, and activities is a valuable asset. Making the most of available resources, such as materials you already have and can rework and adapt quickly for specific classes and needs, is a skill-set to use every day. Even if a teacher doesn't feel inherently creative this is an area that can improve with practice.

4. *Tech-Savvy*–To be technologically savvy is to have a good understanding of modern technology and know how to use it well. In today's highly digital world technology plays a vital role in education overall, and in ESL learning in significant ways, particularly when teaching on Zoom, Google Meet or similar video platforms. Coming to class well prepared is always a must, but now being knowledgeable about these platforms and how to handle various scenarios that may occur when using them almost guarantees a smooth going class. In fact, being tech-savvy shows a new level of teacher professionalism that wasn't considered a decade ago.

5. *Commitment to Learning*–As the world and technology evolve and grow, it's important for teachers to be proactive and continually learning. Long time fundamental teaching methods are changing or being pushed aside by newer trends. Commitment to learning should include not only ESL teacher professional development like classes, workshops, conferences, seminars, and webinars, but also staying current on evolving student demographics: ethnic and cultural diversity, learning goals, and English proficiency. It's crucial for teachers to adapt and embrace new technology and teaching methods to remain up to date.

Adult ESL Teacher Success

Get it right

MANY OF THE ATTRIBUTES of a great ESL teacher are built on the foundation of a well prepared adult education teacher.

In addition to formal qualifications, including education and certification requirements for teaching adult ESL, there are unique qualities that define successful ESL teachers. While most qualities that make good teachers are the same no matter what the subject  taught is, ESL teachers in particular work with international learners, which adds another layer of skill-set to teacher success. Adult ESL learners especially need and expect lessons relevant to their needs.

ESL teachers have training in second language acquisition and techniques for teaching adult learners. Working with adult learners is a specialized teaching area that recognizes the life skills adult learners bring to the classroom. Unlike pedagogy, the art and science of teaching children, adults learn in other ways termed Adult Learning Theory, known as *andragogy,* a philosophy of teaching methods specific to adults. The term was first introduced by Alexander Kapp, a German high school teacher, in 1833. Though the interest in adult learning has a long history, the term andragogy was popularized in North America by Malcolm Knowles, an adult educator, in 1968.

Andragogy refers to the strategies and theories based on the humanistic approach to learning, effective methodologies for helping adults learn. The idea of helping people learn, or self-directed learning, is fundamental as adult learners build on what they already know. In his research on the the ways adults learn, Knowles developed the five assumptions underlying andragogy.

1. *Self-Direction*–As a person matures his or her self-concept is increasingly moving from a dependent personality to one of being self-directed to have ownership of what and how to learn.

2. *Life Experience*–An adult accumulates experience which is a fertile resource for learning. Most adults have rich life experiences that can integrate with new knowledge as they reference what they have done or already know.

3. *Readiness to Learn*–The notion of readiness implies an internal state of being psychologically ready for self-directed learning, meaning adults are more selective about the information they take in. Adults want to learn what is relevant and useful to them now or for the job or skill they want soon.

4. *Orientation to Learn*–As people mature there is a change from future application of knowledge to immedi-

ate application. Adults are more problem-centered than subject-centered, and focus on problem solving knowledge and developing relevant skills.

5. Internal Motivation–Adults are motivated to learn by internal rather than external factors. This motivation comes from internal incentives, such as preparing for a new job or job skill, or curiosity like learning another language or new sport for fun.

These five assumptions, all of which are characteristics of the adult learner, form the bases of *andragogy*, the best known theory of adult education.

Adult learners require respect:

- Respect the life experience learners bring to class: Combine new learning with what they already know.

- Ask their opinions: Be open to different perspectives.

- Be mindful of individual learning styles: Adults need to learn in their own ways.

- Let them talk: Maximize learner talk time to share ideas, solve problems, ask questions.

Notes to Teacher

- *Adults often face many challenges to learning,* such as limited time, financial barriers, self doubt, learning difficulties, and lack of support. Most of these issues are shared by other adults who want or need to learn something new for a myriad of reasons: to do a new job, gain new skills or increase existing ones, fill knowledge gaps, learn a hobby or craft, or reenter the job market after a divorce. Qualified adult education teachers know and respect these aspects as important points to keep in mind for creating curriculum in a welcoming learning environment so adults can reach their goals with confidence.

- *Learners must be motivated before any learning happens.* To this end they must see a need for acquiring knowledge that results from their study. While internal factors are pushing the learner, there can be external factors as well. Often these external factors are evident in business learners sent to the United States to study English. Frequently they have to learn in order to comply with the expectations of a job, company, or someone else with authority that they need to please. Unfortunately, such responsibility might create barriers to learning. Knowing why learners are there can greatly help the teaching process. Though some learners are driven to learn under pressure, some others are not and may become resentful or even resistant to learning. In all situations teachers can be helpful when they take time to find out about learners' reasons for studying.

- *Additionally, because adults learn in different ways,* a teacher should aim to provide learners with opportunities to learn in ways that suit their particular learning styles. In this way learners can feel better empowered with a range of learning strategies to have autonomy in learning the target language. Everyone does not learn in the same way or at the same pace. Self-direction is very important for adult learning because learners will need to use their new language skills outside the classroom.

- *Varied learning strategies* allow learners the autonomy to learn through their own initiatives. Adult learning styles are categorized as: *visual, auditory, linguistic, logical, kinesthetic, intrapersonal, and interpersonal,* though a few more can be present. Teachers should research these different learning styles to tailor lesson methods and strategies to use with learners in group and private classes.

Well structured lessons with clear, relatable objectives that fit student needs are top of the list. What are the lesson goals to validate time spent in class?

- *Have a need based approach* –Learners want to know why they need to know what they are learning.

- *Present the benefits* –Each learner will ask, "How does this information benefit me?"

- *Immediacy* –Show how to use learning. Learners want to see how what they are learning will benefit them now.

- *Active learning* –Engagement. Learners enjoy and learn from activities and games where they interact in fluency and listening practice.

Note: In recent years there has been increased focus and discussion on lifelong learning, the adult learner, and andragogy. While andragogy remains a respected and referred–to paradigm, there have been more questions on a range of adult education issues, from the amount of available time and money adults have for self-directed learning (or whether adults always want self-directed educational experiences) to thoughts on pedagogy vs andragogy in practice. Learning theories continue to evolve and influence education. Readers can research more on andragogy and the adult learner.

Motivation to Learn

Need it, learn it, use it!

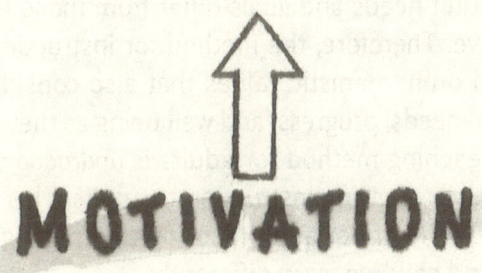

MOTIVATION

ENGLISH LANGUAGE ABILITY is now a required skill in the international business world, although not exclusively. From research on why students choose a particular FL to learn, several trends emerged. Of the factors that affected language selection, employment opportunity was a top reason to study a specific language, followed by its economic importance, learner affinity for the culture, and desire to travel.

Plus, in an increasingly globalized, interconnected world many people see how learning a second (L2) or third language (L3) can be an asset, or even a necessity. Proficiency in another language can offer personal and professional opportunities. Certainly, economic considerations play a major role in influencing FL choice for international business students. Additional benefits include cultural understanding and awareness, deeper respect for diversity, and again a competitive edge in job markets where FL skills break down linguistic barriers.

———*ele*———

Many international adult learners come to the United States to study English and enter the classroom with specific needs and goals that fit their particular life situations. These adult needs and goals differ from those that children have. Therefore, the method for instructing adults is based on humanistic values that also consider adult learners' needs, progress, and well being as they learn.

The teaching method for adults is *andragogy*, the art and science of giving instruction to adults. This method refers to a theory of adult learning that highlights how adults and children learn differently.

Motivation First

The journey to FL proficiency has its ups and downs, and not everyone is as adept at language learning as others. While motivation is the key to learning just about anything, several other factors work together.

Of the five assumptions underlying andragogy, internal motivation is considered as one very important factor that shapes an adult learner's attitude toward learning. This drive to learn comes from an internal stimulation and inquisitiveness, as opposed to external factors such as parental or government requirements to learn information. This internal motivation is a core element of adult learning.

Within the area of motivation, self-assessment is a valuable tool as well. Language learners can often assess their own learning in pretty accurate ways. Self-assessment is important for learners because it encourages them to reflect on their own learning progress and recognize their strengths and weaknesses. This process can help learners evaluate areas they do well in and areas that need improvement.

Researchers have found that learner anxiety, too, plays a role in self assessment, and anxious learners tend to underestimate their L2 competency while less anxious learners tend to overestimate their competency levels. Overestimation may not be much of a problem since it can increase a learner's willingness to go out and communicate. On the flip side, learners that underestimate their L2 ability may be reassured when they interact positively with native speakers. Learners use their abilities to self-assess continually throughout their studies. Success is encouragement to continue learning. Clearly, learner self-assessment aligns with adult learner autonomy and self-directed learning.

Afterword

Time in the real world

THIS BOOK BRINGS THE stories behind the story. It tells the learner stories behind the teacher story of my multi-layered experience teaching ESL.

The world of ESL comes to life through anecdotes that further answer the questions *why are they here?* and *what's the purpose?* put forward in the front pages of this book.

Since people have many different reasons for learning English and for taking the courses that they choose, ESL teachers must be flexible and culturally sensitive to create a class environment that encourages student learning.

Everyday Times

After I earned my master's degree I continued working as a graphic artist while teaching part time until circumstances changed that pushed me into teaching full time. Honestly, full time teaching took its toll on me. Just when I thought, "I can't do this another day," the alarm would go off and I'd get up to do it again. Fortunately, my creativity always saved my spirits; it was my lifeline, my comfort.

Time to Reflect

I wish I had the perfect set of tips on how to avoid stressful situations for ESL teachers. I may not have the perfect set of tips, but I have a few.

For starters, knowing the difference in employment at colleges and universities versus private ESL schools would give teachers insight into who their best employer could be, and might save them from disappointment as well.

Generally speaking, colleges and universities are great for experienced teachers and pay considerably higher rates than private schools. These schools also recruit teachers with higher educational backgrounds, often require teachers to have master's degrees, and have them work fewer hours than at private ESL schools.

Many private ESL schools are actually chains or franchises of larger businesses. These schools often come with a specific way of teaching plus brand loyalty that continues to attract customers who are its students. A school earns its brand loyalty from its particular learning method–remember, the school is a *business* and its school model is what drives its profit.

Another type of private ESL school is individually owned, often run by entrepreneurs or educators, who may also be co-owners. ESL school owners have a passion for languages and learning and have studied a foreign language or worked as teachers themselves. Although well aware that their students are the school's livelihood, these owners are ambitious business people who may work hard to maintain their school's profit.

The foundation of these and all schools should be a well defined mission: the school's purpose or objectives. As a teacher you can ask to know your school's mission goals and check that these ideals are met.

Over the years I have learned so much through a gamut of teaching experiences, from uplifting to upsetting. The sum of it all has culminated into one piece of advice for me to pass along: simply trust your gut and listen to your inner voice. Ultimately, it is important to be mindful of the goings on at your school and what you, the teacher, are asked or expected to do, including being made to continue work through lunch, break times, or other "extras" without additional pay. Regulations governing private school teacher compensation vary state by state, so check local laws for the specifics.

The problems are particularly evident and hard to challenge at ESL schools abroad, in Asia in particular. However, most teachers who have taught abroad say all in all the experience was worth it for reasons too many to list. But before signing on research the school, do an online search at minimum and if possible look for teacher reviews on working at the school before making the jump overseas. *Note:* there are a number of informative and useful online blogs under titles highlighting being an ESL teacher abroad or asking if teaching English abroad is worth it, so take some time to educate yourself. Zero in on the country you want to teach in for information to help you decide.

The Best of Times

I have taught all levels of ESL and especially enjoyed teaching business English, sometimes termed *English for Professional Development,* for the opportunity to work with international professionals. I became known for my business English teaching skills and ability to create targeted lessons. In addition to teaching at several schools over the years, I also worked with a few out-of-state schools and language training agencies as an on-site ESL instructor. One agency assigned me a number of clients primarily at a biotechnology corporation, an industry leader, where I worked for more than five years with an incredible group of international doctors, pharmacists, chemists, scientists, tech pros, and others. Those wonderfully enriching teaching moments became meaningful connections and forever memories.

The Worst of Times

Fortunately, the majority of schools I have worked with have been positive experiences. I can report one negative, though horribly negative, experience well into my time at the school that in the end became a classic *turning lemons into lemonade* opportunity for justice. The phrase is a cliché, I know, and though I loathe clichés it works perfectly here.

Individually owned ESL schools are run on the whims of their owners–a group of entrepreneurs or educators, sometimes co-owners. These owners are driven to control their projects that must generate revenue to be viable, which gives an underlying vibe to the school and how teachers and staff feel there.

This last story is my personal experience of when I took action against a toxic ESL school situation.

I had been working at a privately owned ESL school for about six years when some festering internal squabbling between the owners and school directors manifested to firing both the school's academic director and school director, two well liked and capable professionals. These abrupt firings shocked the teachers, who had no idea why these two excellent people were treated so badly. Plus, the shock broadened when an awkwardly inept young woman quickly replaced the academic director, and a middling teacher immediately went after the director's job.

Dismissals didn't stop there. One odd firing was of a female teacher pulled from her class mid-way and replaced with another teacher to finish. What would the students think?

Early one evening a few weeks after the two director firings I saw the new directors pacing by the teachers' room where I was preparing to leave, their eyes darting as if to see that everyone else had left. They hadn't; one co-teacher was in a back classroom. The new directors, like two sinister witches, angrily called me out of the teachers' room, pointing to the director's office and screamed for me to get into the room. I told them not to speak to me that way as I was leaving, but they continued to point to the office. Inside the director locked the door, told me to sit, and then fired me. I asked why I was being fired but she said it was confidential. My brain was momentarily confused. *Confidential?* Seriously? I quietly snickered in disbelief.

The director said in consideration of my many years teaching there in addition to my wages I would receive a small severance pay. She then shoved a stapled wad of paper toward me and said to take it home, read it, sign and mail it back. I gathered my belongings and left the school, taking the stapled papers with me.

At home I read the papers, and as I had expected, saw too much I couldn't agree to or even cross out. Notably, I could not talk about the goings on at the school, speak negatively of it, or share any information I had from my time working there. I knew I wasn't signing. This attempt to silence me with a bit of payout backfired on the school, its owner, and directors.

I soon came to suspect that I was let go due to a brief email chat I had with a co-teacher about the school not closing on one federal holiday. Some students knew about the holiday and asked us why they didn't get the day off; we teachers didn't have a satisfactory answer though we agreed with the students. This chat was an aside from our main lesson discussion on the school's email that was monitored by school management, though, unfortunately, my co-teacher and I hadn't thought of that caveat then.

For years, teachers at our school faced ongoing exploitation, often going uncompensated for work they completed outside of regular work hours. For example, teachers were required to attend weekly graduations scheduled during their lunch breaks, and to fill out student evaluation forms and extensive assessments for private and business students, typically done after hours and at home. In addition, teachers dedicated significant evening or weekend time, without pay, to essential daily lesson preparations. This "prep time" also included creating tests or quizzes—often on a weekly basis— and subsequent grading them for each student. It was particularly frustrating that the school consistently refused to compensate teachers for this vital work on personal time.

The school firings and subsequent attempts to remove and silence me, a long time teacher, with a bit of money and warnings initially upset me, but then ignited an urgency to take action to speak truth and help effect change for current and future teachers. To this end I took legal action against the school. With a former school staff member as a witness I won my legal case. My win ultimately brought about change to benefit all teachers at the school, which was a well deserved goal.

Acknowledgments

Thank You!

IT MAY NOT TAKE an entire village to write a memoir in an offbeat, witty yet serious writing style, but heartfelt thanks are due to my enthusiastic supporters who helped bring this distinctive book to life. To all those who have helped make my little book dream a reality, I am incredibly grateful.

Huge thanks to author Robert Graysmith for his unwavering support for my unconventional and somewhat quirky story telling style. His excitement for this project was evident from the start. With an artist's eye, he was a great help whenever I asked, "This one or that one?" as I showed one illustration or another. From his thumbs up reaction I could make the right decision.

Thanks to Aaron Smith for helping to navigate the new-to-me publishing maze, and unlock its hidden parts when I had no idea.

A special thank you to Margot Graysmith for her meticulous feedback on my evolving book cover, encouragement throughout my writing, and determined faith that I would soon be a published author—you are the best.

With great appreciation to Martin Wininger, grammarian of note and fellow ESL teacher for helping to clarify some school time gaps, being there to discuss a grammar point or two, and in his own words, "Well, that's my two-cents' worth."

Thanks to fellow writer-film maker the late Jo Lauer for her self publishing tips that helped me anticipate the steps ahead to be better prepared.

And finally to all my students, fellow teachers, helpful school staff, and international professionals I had the pleasure to work with at small and large venues over the years, I truly appreciate you. Thank you for sharing your hopes, fears, struggles, and dreams with me, and of course, for the laughter we had together. Above all, thanks for the memories you helped me shape into stories on these pages.

Background pattern by Freepik

About the Author

Just between us

MELANIE GRAYSMITH is a writer, artist, and educator with a passion for creativity in all forms; she turns mere interests into serious study. Her lifetime love of language and culture led to degrees in art, Japanese, and education and a career shaped by storytelling. Whether writing short stories, poetry, or screenplays, Melanie brings creative depth to every project. She is also an longtime active member of the Bay Area independent film community. *What The ESL:* is her first published book.

A significant time in Melanie's life was portrayed by actress Chloë Sevigny in the praised Hollywood film *Zodiac*, from director David Fincher. Melanie was also a consultant on the film. She lives in San Francisco where she writes, teaches, and creates visual art.

The ABeCeDarian ESL learner is...

Ambitious
Bold
Confident
Determined,
Encouraged
Focused
Gainful
Hardworking
Inquisitive
Joyful
Keen
Limitless
Motivated
Nervy
Observant
Positive
Quick
Resourceful
Stimulated
Tenacious
Unafraid
Voracious
Wondering
Xenacious
Yearning
Zestful

Feedback Request

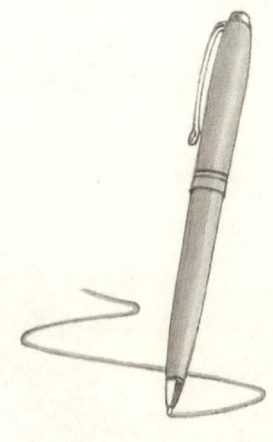

If you enjoyed this book, please send in a review as I would appreciate your feedback.

Send your thoughts to: melaniegwrites@gmail.com

Reviews can help readers discover this book and support my work. Your opinion lets me know how readers enjoyed the book or how it can be improved.

Thank you for taking the time to share your feedback. It is important and much appreciated!

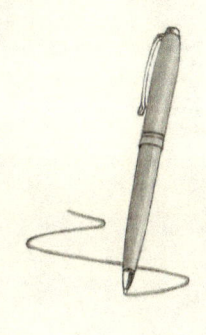

www.ingramcontent.com/pod-product-compliance
Lightning Source LLC
Chambersburg PA
CBHW021113130626
46554CB00002B/667